AMERICA IN THE TIME OF
GEORGE WASHINGTON

1747 to 1803

Sally Senzell Isaacs

Heinemann Library
Des Plaines, Illinois

Published by Heinemann Library,
an imprint of Reed Educational & Professional Publishing,
1350 East Touhy Avenue, Suite 240 West
Des Plaines, IL 60018.

AMERICA IN THE TIME OF GEORGE WASHINGTON
was produced for Heinemann Library
by Bender Richardson White.

Editor: Lionel Bender
Designer: Ben White
Assistant Editor: Michael March
Picture Researcher: Madeleine Samuel
Media Conversion and Typesetting: MW Graphics
Production Controller: Kim Richardson

03 02 01 00
10 9 8 7 6 5 4 3

Printed in Hong Kong

Library of Congress Cataloging-in-Publication Data.
Isaacs, Sally, 1950–
    America in the time of George Washington : 1747 to 1803 / Sally
Senzell Isaacs.
        p.   cm.
    Includes bibliographical references and index.
    Summary: Uses the life of George Washington as a reference to
examine the history of the United States during the French and Indian War,
the Revolutionary War, the time of the Continental Congress, and early
years of this new nation.
    ISBN 1-57572-743-9 (lib. bdg.)   ISBN 1-57572-934-2 (pbk.)
    1. United States--History--Revolution, 1775-1783--Juvenile literature.
2. United States--History--1783-1815--Juvenile literature. 3. United
States--History--Colonial period, ca.1600-1775--Juvenile literature.
4. Washington, George, 1732-1799--Juvenile literature. [1. United
States--History--Revolution,1775-1783. 2. United States--History--1783-
1815. 3. United States--History--Colonial period, ca.1600-1775.
4. Washington, George, 1732-1799.]   I. Title.
E208.I63   1998
973--dc21   98-34220
                                                         CIP
                                                          AC

Special thanks to Mike Carpenter, Scott Westerfield, and Tristan Boyer at
Heinemann Library for editorial and design guidance and direction.

Photo Credits:
Picture Research Consultants, Massachusetts: pages 8 (Library of
Congress), 11 (Library of Congress), 12 bottom (John Carter Brown
Library), 14 (Library of Congress), 15 (Concord Museum), 16 (Library of
Congress), 19 bottom, 22 (Private Collection), 25 bottom (West
Point/photographer Josh Nefsky), 29 top (Bucks County Historical Society),
33 (The New York Public Library/Astor, Lenox and Tilden Foundation), 35
(Smithsonian Institute/Kim Nielsen), 37 (Library of Congress), 41
(Smithsonian Institute). Peter Newark's American Pictures: pages 7 top, 9,
10, 12 top, 17, 21, 23, 27, 29 bottom, 30, 31, 32, 34, 36, 38, 40. North
Wind Picture Archives: pages 7 bottom, 19 top, 25 top, 39.

Artwork credits
Illustrations by: John James on pages 6/7, 10/11, 12/13, 14/15, 18/19,
24/25, 30/31, 34/35, 36/37, 40/41; Mark Bergin on pages 8/9, 20/21,
32/33, 38/39; Gerald Wood on pages 16/17, 26/27; Nick Hewetson on
pages 22/23, 28/29. Maps by Stefan Chabluk.
Cover: Design and make-up by Pelican Graphics. Artwork by John James.
Photos: Top: North Wind Picture Archives. Center and bottom: Picture
Research Consultants (Library of Congress).

Major quotations used in this book come from the following
sources. Some of the quotations have been abridged for
clarity:
Page 12: Stamp Act Congress – *Documents of American
History* - 6th Edition. New York: Commager Press. Pages
57–58.
Page 16: Samuel Adam's quote: From *The Massachusetts
Colony* by Dennis Fradin. Chicago: Children's Press, 1987.
Page 125.
Page 20: Patrick Henry's speech. There is no written
record of the speech. It was printed in an early biography
of Henry by William Wirt, who relied on accounts given to
him by people who heard the speech.
Page 24: Quote by Joseph Martin, private in First
Connecticut Brigade. Written in 1830 in *A Narrative of
Some of the Adventures, Dangers, and Suffering of a
Revolutionary War Soldier*. Reprinted in *A Soldier At
Morristown*. Gettysburg: Thomas Publications, P.O. Box
3031, PA 17325—Eastern National Park and Monument
Association, 1978.
Page 34: Frederick Law Olmsted quote from *Slavery in
America* by Robert Liston. New York: McGraw Hill Book
Company, 1970. Page 71.
Page 37: Tecumseh's words from *Native American
Testimony*, edited by Peter Nabokov. New York: Thomas
Y. Crowell, 1978. Page 119.

The Consultants
Special thanks go to Diane Smolinski and
Nancy Cope for their help in the preparation of
this series. Diane Smolinski has years of
experience interpreting standards documents
and putting them into practice in fourth and fifth
grade classrooms. Nancy Cope splits her time
between teaching high school history, chairing
her department, training new teachers at North
Carolina State University, and being President-
Elect of the North Carolina Council
for Social Studies.

The Author
Sally Senzell Isaacs is a professional writer
and editor of nonfiction books for children.
She graduated from Indiana University, earning a
B.S. degree in Education with majors in
American History and Sociology. For some
years, she was the Editorial Director of
Reader's Digest Educational Division. Sally
Senzell Isaacs lives in New Jersey with her
husband and two children.

CONTENTS

America in the Time of is a series of nine books arranged chronologically, meaning that events are described in the order in which they happened. However, since each book focuses on an important person in American history, the timespans of the titles overlap. In each book, most articles deal with a particular event or part of American history. Others deal with aspects of everyday life, such as trade, houses, clothing, and farming. These general articles cover longer periods of time. The little illustrations at the top left of each article are a symbol of the times. They are identified on page 3.

▼ **About the map**

This map shows the United States today. It shows the boundaries and names of all the states. Refer to this map, or to the one on pages 42–43, to locate places talked about in this book.

About this book

This book is about America from 1747 to 1803—as the nation began to take shape with the help of George Washington. The term America means "the United States of America." The term British refers to the people and things of England or Great Britain. In 1707, Scotland joined England and Wales to form the country of Great Britain. Usually, we refer to the native people of America as Native Americans. But occasionally we call them Indians, as Christopher Columbus did when he arrived in America in 1492. Words in **bold** are described in more detail in the glossary on page 46.

INTRODUCTION

This book tells how a small group of English colonies became the United States of America. George Washington played an especially important part in this process. He helped shape the country in three major ways. First, he commanded the Continental Army that fought for independence from Britain. Second, he was president of the **convention**, or group of people, that wrote the United States **Constitution**. Third, he was the first president of the United States.

During this time, it seemed as if America was becoming "the land of the free." This was not exactly true. Freedom was a stranger to many people in America. Native Americans were rapidly losing the freedom to live on their own land. Africans lost their freedom when they were captured in their native land and sold as **slaves** to work on American farms. Among the European settlers, women did not even share the freedom held by the men. They did not have the rights to vote and own land.

Most of the events described and illustrated in the book took place during George Washington's life. Other events happened after he died. On many of the pages that describe events during Washington's life, there are yellow boxes that tell you what he or his family was doing at the time.

YOUNG GEORGE WASHINGTON

While most of America was still wilderness, George Washington was growing up in the colony of Virginia. There were 13 colonies in America, all governed by Britain. Virginia was the oldest colony. By the time Washington was born, many Virginians lived in comfortable homes with large farms.

George Washington was born on February 22, 1732. He spent most of his boyhood years on a **plantation** called Ferry Farm near Fredericksburg, Virginia. Historians are uncertain where he attended school. By looking at his old notebooks, it seems that George learned math, geography, and some Latin. Historians agree that George did not attend school after the age of 15.

▼ Tobacco was grown on Ferry Farm. Tobacco leaves were snapped off the stalks, dried, and later loaded into shipping barrels. When George was 11 years old, his father died. George became owner of Ferry Farm and the 20 African slaves who worked there. George helped his mother run the farm.

How the Washingtons came to Virginia

George's family came from England to the colonies by accident. In the 1650s, his great-grandfather, John, was working on an English ship. The ship ran aground in the Potomac River. John looked around the Virginia colony and decided to settle there. George's father was Augustine Washington. His mother was Mary Ball Washington.

George was actually born on February 11, 1732. In 1752, America changed from using the Julian to the Gregorian calender. Eleven days were lost from that year. That is why we now celebrate Washington's birthday on February 22.

As a surveyor, George measured and marked out land. People hired him to help them divide up and sell land. At first, George worked near his farm. Then he surveyed the Shenandoah River valley and the wilderness west of Virginia. In July 1749, George Washington was made official surveyor for Culpeper County in Virginia.

At age 20, George Washington joined the Virginia **militia**, a group of volunteer soldiers. This picture, painted by Charles Willson Peale, shows him in 1754 as a colonel of the militia.

During battles with the French, the people of Virginia sought help from Washington and his forces. In this **engraving** of 1755, Washington is shown on horseback.

From surveyor to soldier

When George was old enough to get a job, he really wanted to be an explorer. He dreamed of sailing ships for the British Royal **Navy**. His mother, however, would not let him go so far from home. So, George became a surveyor at age 16. If he could not explore the seas, he would explore the unsettled **frontier** west of Virginia. The land was muddy and wooded. George loved the adventure of sleeping outside and cooking over a campfire.

At age 20, George started his **military** career. At this time, there was a vast area of land west of the 13 colonies, called Ohio country. French explorers had **claimed** this land for France. Since the British owned the 13 colonies, they wanted to own the western land, too.

At first, George delivered messages between the French and the British. Then, in April 1754, he led British troops into battle at the start of what was to become a long war with the French.

JOIN or DIE

THE FRENCH AND INDIAN WAR

America had become a gameboard. Spain, France, and Great Britain placed their markers at various places. Great Britain owned the 13 colonies and northern Canada. Spain claimed the West and Florida. France claimed a vast area in the middle, plus lower Canada.

In 1754, France and Great Britain started to fight over America. Great Britain wanted the land beside the Mississippi and Ohio rivers. Its colonies were growing and its settlers wanted to move west. It tried to take away land from the French as well as from Native Americans. Many Native Americans decided to help the French fight the British. That is why colonists named the nine-year battle the French and Indian War. The war spread to Europe in 1756. People there called it the Seven Years War.

Timeline of the War
1754 the French and Indian War begins. George Washington, commander of about 150 men, loses battle at Fort Necessity
1756 the war spreads to Europe
1757 the French capture Fort Oswego on Lake Ontario and Fort William Henry on Lake George
1757 William Pitt becomes Great Britain's Prime Minister and turns the battle in Britain's favor
1759 the British capture Quebec
1760 the British capture Montreal
1762 Spain enters the war on the French side.
1763 Great Britain and France sign the Treaty of Paris to end the war. The treaty gave Britain almost all of Canada and French land east of the Mississippi River.

► The war was fought on land and in the water. Here, a French ship (in the foreground) carrying troops and supplies is fired on by a British ship as it tries to enter the St. Lawrence River. The French needed to protect their important river settlements of Quebec and Montreal.

▼ This painting shows the taking of Quebec City in Canada by 30,000 British troops on September 13, 1759. The British forces arrived in 168 ships.

At first, the British lost several battles. Their general, Edward Braddock, knew how to fight in Europe, but not in the forests of America.

George Washington was part of Braddock's troops. He wrote about a surprise attack by the French and Indians: "The English soldiers broke and ran as sheep before the hounds. The general was wounded. He died three days after. I luckily escaped without a wound...."

▲ This Iroquois warrior carries the scalp of a British soldier on the barrel of his musket. This watercolor was painted in 1787.

The British start to win

In 1758, the British gathered many more colonial soldiers to fight the French. They also persuaded some Native American tribes to join them. In 1759, they beat the French at Quebec. In 1760, they took control of Montreal. Without them, the French could no longer supply their forts along the St. Lawrence River.

In 1763, Great Britain and France signed a **treaty** to end the war. France gave up all land east of the Mississippi River. They also gave up their land in Canada. They had already given their land west of the Mississippi to Spain in return for Spain's help in the war. Now Great Britain and Spain **claimed** most of North America.

◀ British soldiers—in bright red jackets—did not know how to fight in forests of North America. The French and Indians attacked them by surprise. Later, with better leaders, the British started to win the war.

9

TAXES

Britain's King George III had a big problem after the French and Indian War. His government needed money. The war had been very costly. One solution was popular in his country: Let's make the colonies give us more money! After all, Great Britain went to great expense to protect the colonies during the war.

▲ This drawing in a newspaper of 1765 shows the colonists' hate for the Stamp Act.

Great Britain made colonists in America pay a **tax** whenever they bought certain things. The tax was extra money added to the normal price. The extra money was sent back to Britain. First a tax on sugar and molasses was passed in 1764.

The British government sent many officials to the colonies to make sure taxes were paid. The officials were allowed to search colonists' homes and stores for goods that might have been **smuggled** into the colonies without paying taxes. The colonists hated the tax and the searches. All British citizens had a right to privacy in their homes. Colonists were no longer being treated as British citizens by the government!

Yet another tax

The Stamp Act was passed in 1765. Colonists now had to pay a tax on such items as newspapers, calendars, playing cards, and almanacs. A stamp was put on each item to show the tax was paid.

Colonists were furious! They could not vote to elect **representatives** to Britain's government (called **Parliament**). Yet Parliament could make laws about the colonies. Colonists poured into the streets to **protest.** Tax collectors were chased out of town. In 1766, the Stamp Act was removed, but the argument over taxes was not over. The colonists said they would pay taxes only if their own elected governments passed a tax act.

◄ An English magazine cartoon of the time shows the **repeal** of the American Stamp Act on March 18, 1766. The cartoon, called *The Funeral of Ame Stamp*, shows Members of Parliament in Britain crying over the loss of taxes from America. It also shows English ships having unloaded stamps and goods from America.

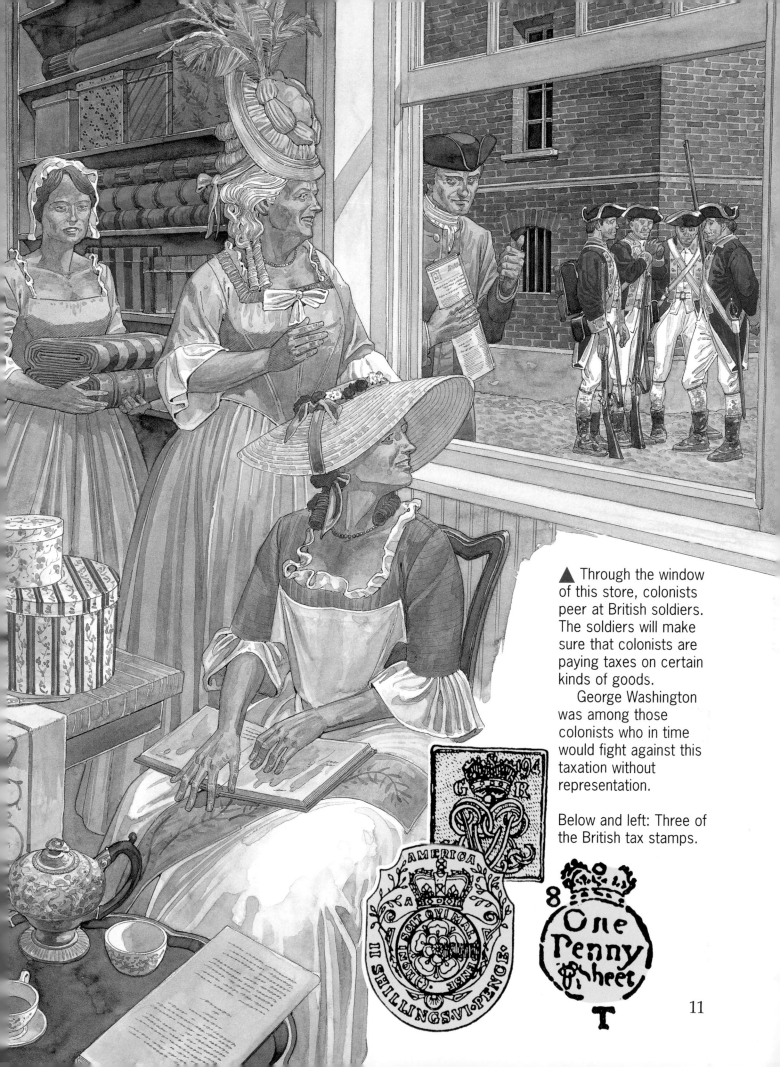

▲ Through the window of this store, colonists peer at British soldiers. The soldiers will make sure that colonists are paying taxes on certain kinds of goods.

George Washington was among those colonists who in time would fight against this taxation without representation.

Below and left: Three of the British tax stamps.

11

SONS AND DAUGHTERS OF LIBERTY

Never before had colonists acted together against the British government. Now, however, people of colonies stretching from New Hampshire to Georgia were agreed. They must work together to get their message across to Britain's king. The taxes must be stopped.

In 1765, citizens from nine colonies met at the Stamp Act **Congress**. They wrote to the British government: "It is inseparably essential to the freedom of a people, and the undoubted right of Englishmen, that no taxes be imposed on them but with their own consent given personally or by their **representatives**."

Other colonists were not satisfied with writing documents. They formed a group called the Sons of Liberty. They told colonists to boycott, or stop buying, British goods. A group of women called the Daughters of Liberty joined the action. They stopped wearing dresses made from British cloth. They worked together to weave homemade cloth.

Washington's opinion
In 1758, George Washington was first elected as a representative to Virginia's government called the **House of Burgesses**. The House encouraged the boycott of British goods. While he still felt loyal to the British government, Washington was one of the first American leaders to suggest the use of force to protect America's liberty.

In a letter to his friend, George Mason, Washington said, "No man should hesitate to use arms in defense of so valuable a blessing. Yet arms should be the last resort."

▲ Phillis Wheatley was one of the most famous poets in the colonies. She came to Boston on a slave ship when she was eight years old. In 1773, her poems were printed by a London publisher. She became the first African American to have a book published.

A constant conflict

British merchants were losing money. The colonists were making their own goods instead of buying from them. Britain **repealed** the Stamp Act in 1766. However, the next year it announced new taxes. The Sons and Daughters of Liberty worked even harder to make sure no one bought British goods.

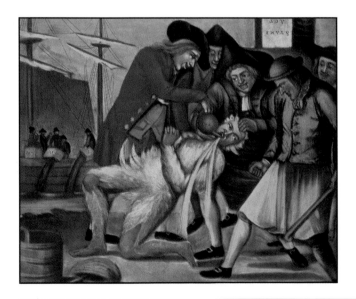

◀ Angry colonists in Boston punish a British tax official by covering him with tar and feathers and forcing him to drink lots of tea.

◄ Life goes on as **protests** swirl through the streets of Boston. In the first floor parlor, or reception room, of a wealthy landowner's townhouse, Sons of Liberly discuss the best way to make Britain repeal the taxes. Upstairs on the second floor, Daughters of Liberty spin thread for making homemade cloth. Other rooms in the house include:
1. servants' bedrooms
2. the householder family's bedrooms
3. dining room
4. parlor
5. kitchen and eating area for servants.

THE BOSTON MASSACRE

Everyone in Boston could feel the tension. Colonists were furious over the taxes. Many secretly smuggled in goods to avoid paying the tax. Great Britain sent over more soldiers to catch the smugglers. Colonists harassed the soldiers by shouting insults, throwing rocks, and covering them with tar and feathers.

On March 5, 1770, things got totally out of control. British soldiers, called redcoats because of the color of their uniforms, were guarding Boston's Customs House. **Tax** money was stored here. A group of angry colonists began shouting and throwing rocks at them. A soldier was knocked down. Someone fired a shot. The redcoats panicked and began shooting the colonists. Five colonists died and seven were wounded.

▼ (Below left) This **engraving** was made by Paul Revere soon after the Boston Massacre. It spread the news and the anger of the event. Revere knew the picture did not tell the truth about what happened in Boston. The British soldiers did not stand right in front of the colonists and shoot them. Yet this picture caught the emotions of colonists everywhere. It made them hate the British even more and helped start the Revolutionary War.

Where is George Washington?
At this time, George Washington is still a **representative** in the **House of Burgesses** and a landowner. By now, he is living at Mount Vernon in Virginia. This was his father's **plantation** which George inherited when his brother died. George lived at Mount Vernon with his wife, Martha, and her two children, Jack and Patsy. George was a careful and successful businessman, investing in a flour mill and reading all he could about farming.

British soldiers train on Boston Common. The townsfolk walk across the Common. This painting was made in 1768 by Christian Remick. Near the Common, the Old State House still stands. Built in 1713, this is Boston's oldest building. Before the Revolution, British officials governed the colonies from here. In 1776, the Declaration of Independence was read to Bostonians from its balcony.

Horrible treatment of the colonists

The fight at the Customs House was reported throughout the colonies. Colonists such as Samuel Adams exaggerated the event into something huge. As soon as the fighting ended at the Customs House, he wrote articles about it, calling it the Boston Massacre.

There were, of course, two sides to the story. Some redcoats claimed they heard someone shout "Fire!" Others said they heard "Hold your fire!" Regardless of what happened, the colonists were angry.

Crispus Attucks was one of the five men killed in the Boston Massacre. He was probably the first colonist killed by the British army. Attucks was a 47-year-old African American runaway slave and a member of the Sons of Liberty.

BOSTON TEA PARTY

Before now, most colonists saw themselves as British citizens. But by 1773, they were calling themselves citizens of the 13 colonies—of Virginia, New York, Massachusetts, and so on. Furthermore, colonists were talking about fighting against Britain, if necessary.

"This meeting can do nothing more to save the country!" said Samuel Adams on December 16, 1773. He spoke to a town meeting in Boston. The Tea Act was the latest of Britain's unpopular laws. It was a way of making Americans buy tea from British merchants and putting local merchants out of business.

Fifty members of the Sons of Liberty, disguised as Native Americans, ran to Boston's **harbor**. They boarded British ships and dumped 342 chests of tea into the ocean. This event became known as the Boston Tea Party.

What Washington thought

When he heard of the Boston Tea Party, George Washington disapproved of the colonists' wastefulness. However, when he heard of the Intolerable Acts, he was furious. He and other members of Virginia's **House of Burgesses protested** against the acts so loudly that the British governor forbade them to meet again. They then held secret meetings at the nearby Raleigh Tavern.

▲ On December 16, 1773, Bostonians showed their anger at Britain's rule over them by dumping British tea into the Atlantic Ocean. This picture is a **lithograph** made in the 1800s by a famous art and printing company called Currier and Ives.

▲ The citizens of Boston depended on their harbor. Food and supplies arrived on ships. American goods were shipped out. At least half of the people earned their living by working on ships or at the harbor. When other colonies heard that Boston's harbor was closed, they sent rice, flour, and money to help the Bostonians survive.

▼ British customs officials collected gold from merchant ships as a **tax** on goods transported through Boston Harbor.

The Intolerable Acts

It took several months for the news of the Boston Tea Party to reach Britain. When it did, King George III was angry. To punish the colonists, he closed the port of Boston by anchoring Royal **Navy** ships in the harbor. Thousands more soldiers were sent to Boston. The British government passed other laws that took away the colonists' rights. The colonists called the laws the Intolerable Acts.

▶ This **engraving** of 1770 shows colonial slaves packing tobacco into barrels for shipping to Britain. When Britain introduced the Intolerable Acts, some colonists, including George Washington, threatened to stop all colonial exports to Britain until Boston's Harbor was reopened.

FIRST CONTINENTAL CONGRESS

Massachusetts was suffering under Britain's rules. Leaders of 12 colonies decided to get together and take action. Georgia did not join them. Could this group persuade the king to stop? Could they make a joint decision over colonial rule?

George Washington was a **delegate** from Virginia at the First Continental **Congress** in Philadelphia. It was his first chance to meet with leaders of the other colonies.

The Congress was like a meeting of leaders from different countries. The delegates did not agree on their course of action. Some wanted to politely ask King George to respect their rights. Others were ready to fight. Yet everyone agreed that the colonies must all stick together.

▼ The First Continental Congress met in Philadelphia in September, 1774. Peyton Randolph was elected its **president.** Another delegate, John Adams, from Massachusetts, later became the second president of the United States.

Acts and reactions
1765 The Stamp Act
1766 The Stamp Act repealed
1767 The Townshend Acts (taxes on such things as glass, paper, silk, and tea)
1770 The Boston Massacre
1770 The Townshend Acts repealed (except tea tax)
1773, May The Tea Act
1773, Dec. The Boston Tea Party
1774, May The Intolerable Acts
1774, Sept. the First Continental Congress

▲ Americans who stayed loyal to the king were called Loyalists. This merchant relied on Britain to send him goods to sell. If the colonies became independent, his business might suffer.

▲ A view of Second Street, Philadelphia, in the 1780s. Wagons, horses, and pedestrians mingle on the street. Women sit outside an inn. There were no paved roads until about 1796. Muddy roads were messy and dangerous for horses. Wooden rails were sometimes laid across a muddy road. This made for a very bumpy ride. By 1780, the population of Philadelphia was over 20,000. Most people were English or Welsh colonists.

▲ Americans who wanted the colonies to be free from Britain were called Patriots. About one-third of the colonists were Patriots, one-third were Loyalists, and the rest were undecided.

◀ This **engraving** from 1775 shows a group of North Carolina women **protesting** the **tax** on tea. They call themselves "Society of Patriotic Ladies." The women have written an agreement to stop drinking tea. While some women are signing the agreement, others are emptying containers of tea.

Preparing for emergency action

The First Continental Congress ended with some decisions. The delegates wrote a letter to King George asking him to **repeal** the Intolerable Acts and stop Britain's taxes on the colonies. The delegates also agreed to return to their colonies with this advice: Stop buying British goods and start forming a **militia**—an army of citizens that might be needed to fight in an emergency. At the end of the meeting, the delegates agreed to meet again in May, 1775.

A SHOT HEARD ROUND THE WORLD

"The next gale that sweeps from the north will bring to our ears the clash of resounding arms!" Patrick Henry spoke these words in Virginia on March 23, 1775. He was predicting that war with Britain could not be avoided. In the same speech, he added his now-famous words: "Give me liberty, or give me death!"

The citizens of Massachusetts were preparing for the worst. They collected a large supply of gunpowder in Concord, about 20 miles (32 km) from Boston. When British General Thomas Gage heard this, he rushed 2,000 troops out of Boston. He ordered them first to Lexington to capture colonial leaders. Then he sent them to Concord to steal the gunpowder.

▲ Britain's **redcoats** were well-trained and disciplined. Britain also hired German soldiers. Some Native Americans and American Loyalists joined the redcoats.

▲ Each colony had a **militia**, a group of volunteer soldiers. They were called minutemen as they were expected to be ready to fight at a minute's notice.

▲ The flintlock musket was used in the Revolutionary War. It fired a large lead ball.

The Battle of Lexington

A young boy overheard General Gage's plans. He ran and told a group of the Sons of Liberty. Quickly, Paul Revere, William Dawes, and Samuel Prescott galloped through Massachusetts warning people that the British were coming. Warning lanterns were hung from Boston's Old North Church and churchbells roused **minutemen** from their beds.

The redcoats arrived in Lexington and were met by 70 minutemen, led by Captain John Parker. A shot was fired. Each side said the other side fired first. The outnumbered Americans barely had a chance. After a brief battle, eight Americans and one British soldier were killed. The Revolutionary War had begun.

Concord ★
Revere captured, Dawes turns back
Lexington ★
Prescott joins Revere and Dawes
Arlington ●
Dawes joins Revere
Charles River
Boston

— Revere
— Dawes
— Prescott
★ Battle site

◀ British troops left Boston on April 18, 1775. They reached Lexington the next morning. After a brief battle and victory, they marched to Concord where 300 colonists surprised them. The redcoats retreated back to Boston. All along the way, they were fired at by angry colonists.

▼ A minuteman's wife gives him his musket as he prepares to join the Revolutionary Army. He leaves instantly, abandoning his horse and plow in the field. This illustration was printed by Currier and Ives in 1876. At first, the Revolutionary Army was poorly trained and badly disciplined.

◀ These Americans are firing at British redcoats at Concord. This was America's first serious attack on the British. British casualties were 73 dead and 200 wounded or missing. The Americans lost 49 men, and 44 were wounded or missing. Sixty years later, New England poet Ralph Waldo Emerson called this "the shot heard round the world."

INDEPENDENCE

In May, 1775, the members of the Second Continental Congress met in Philadelphia. All 13 colonies were represented. They faced an enormous decision. Should America declare independence from Great Britain? If they fought a war and lost, they could all be hanged for trying to overthrow the king.

In May, 1775, the Second Continental **Congress** made two important decisions. First, they sent King George a statement of loyalty to him, but asked him to end the Intolerable Acts and the fighting. Their second decision was to form the Continental Army. They chose George Washington to be its commander.

Common Sense
Most colonists were not ready to break away from Great Britain. Thomas Paine helped change their minds. In January, 1776, he wrote a pamphlet called *Common Sense*. He asked why Americans should be ruled by one man living 3,000 miles (4,800 km) away. Colonists began talking about Paine's ideas. Many agreed with him.

The Declaration of Independence
In June, 1776, The Second Continental Congress selected a committee to write a Declaration of Independence. They asked Thomas Jefferson to do most of the writing. After making 80 changes to his draft, the Congress **adopted** the **declaration** on July 4. The American colonies were free from Britain. Britain, however, was not willing to accept this. The colonies would have to earn their independence by winning a war.

▼ This painting by William Walcutt of 1864 shows New Yorkers pulling down a statue of King George III on July 10, 1776.

Washington in command
Congress chose George Washington to lead the Continental Army because of his military experience in the French and Indian War. While his troops had not done very well in that war, Washington had shown that he could train soldiers well, knew how to run an army, and was courageous. Also, he seemed to have an even temper and strong will. However, Washington was nervous about taking the difficult job.

◀ Proud Americans rang this bell on July 8, 1776, when the Declaration of Independence was announced. They rang it each year after that on July 8 until 1835. That year, the bell cracked. The bell has been in Philadelphia since 1752. It was first called the Old State House Bell. Around 1839, people named it the Liberty Bell.

◀ This **engraving** of 1797 by John Trumbull shows the five-member committee presenting the Declaration of Independence to the Congress. Two of the statements made in the document were:
• People have the right to life and liberty, and the right to seek happiness.
• The colonies were breaking away from Great Britain to become the United States of America.

▼ The Declaration of Independence was first read outside the Pennsylvania State House on July 8, 1776. The crowd below celebrated. During the next month, it was read to joyful crowds in towns throughout America.

23

THE REVOLUTIONARY SOLDIER

Word spread through the colonies: Americans had defeated British troops at Concord! In all the colonies, citizens had to decide if they, too, were willing to fight. Thousands were ready. Battles between American and British soldiers broke out in New York, Pennsylvania, the Carolinas, and New Jersey.

George Washington had a difficult job. As commander of the Continental Army, he had to train his men to beat the British soldiers. Until now, men had volunteered as part-time soldiers in their colonial **militia**. They served for a short time, whenever they were needed to defend their communities. Now Washington had to convince men from all the colonies to leave home and join his army.

In August 1776, Washington had about 18,000 soldiers. British General Howe had 41,000. That month, the two sides clashed in New York City. About 400 Americans were killed or wounded, and 1,200 were taken prisoner. The Americans were forced out and New York City remained in British hands for five years.

A new national government
In 1781, the Second Continental **Congress** agreed on the Articles of **Confederation**. This document loosely joined the states together with a national government. The government had little power. It could not collect **taxes**. It had no leader, such as a president. The **states** were afraid of a strong central government. They were afraid that people would lose the right to govern themselves—the very point of the War of Independence with Britain.

▶ After their victories at Trenton and Princeton, New Jersey, the Continental Army spent the winter of 1779–1780 in Morristown, New Jersey.

▶ One of the cabins was set up as a medical hut. With few supplies, doctors had to set broken legs and bring down fevers.

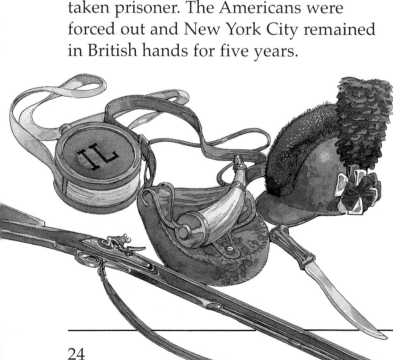

▶ One of Washington's men, ready to fight.

◀ Every soldier in the Continental Army tried to hang onto these essential items: a water bottle, musket, helmet, bullet bag, horn, and knife. The army counted on France, Spain, and the Netherlands for money to buy supplies.

TO ALL BRAVE, HEALTHY, ABLE BODIED, AND WELL
DISPOSED YOUNG MEN,
IN THIS NEIGHBOURHOOD, WHO HAVE ANY INCLINATION TO JOIN THE TROOPS,
NOW RAISING UNDER
GENERAL WASHINGTON,
FOR THE DEFENCE OF THE
LIBERTIES AND INDEPENDENCE
OF THE UNITED STATES,
Against the hostile designs of foreign enemies,

TAKE NOTICE,

▲ A recruitment poster encourages men to join Washington's army to fight for independence.

Who fought, and why?

Many soldiers joined the army because they were promised free land after the war. At first, most states did not allow African Americans in the army, but by 1778, nearly 5,000 were fighting for America's independence. Many slaves were promised freedom in exchange for fighting. Women helped soldiers by making uniforms and blankets, cooking, and caring for the wounded.

◀ This medicine chest, filled with medicine bottles and jars, weighing scales, and surgical instruments, was used by the Continental Army.

At Morristown, the army made their winter camp on a farm. They built 1,000 log huts, each with sleeping shelves for 12 men. George Washington and his wife stayed in a nearby mansion.

THE ROAD TO VICTORY

Once the war began, it was difficult to control. British and Americans soldiers marched and fought through most of the colonies, leaving death and destruction behind. Both sides believed they were fighting for an honorable cause.

▼ The battle at Yorktown lasted 14 days. About 600 British soldiers and 100 American soldiers died fighting. The Americans had heavy guns and more cannons than the British. America won the battle.

For most of the war, the Continental Army was no match for the British. Great Britain's army and **navy** were among the best in the world. But Americans were defending their freedom and homes. This spirit helped them win the war.

Main battles of the war
Apr. 19, 1775 war begins at Lexington and Concord, MA
June 17, 1775 British win at Bunker Hill, MA
Dec. 26, 1776 America wins at Trenton, NJ
Jan. 3, 1777 Americans win at Princeton, NJ
Aug. 16, 1777 British win at Bennington, VT
Oct. 17, 1777 America wins at Saratoga, NY
June 28,1778 no winner at Monmouth, NJ
Aug. 16, 1780 British win at Camden, SC
Jan. 17, 1781 Americans win at Cowpens, SC
Oct. 6-19, 1781 British surrender at Yorktown, VA

Native Americans help both sides
As the Revolutionary War flared in the East, many Americans continued to move their homes westward, pushing out the Native Americans. Some Native Americans helped the British, hoping that would save their own land. Other Native Americans helped the Continental Army.

► French warships blocked the York River, preventing British ships from bringing more troops to Yorktown.

◄ At the Battle of Monmouth, New Jersey, on June 28, 1778, Mary Hays loaded a cannon in place of her wounded husband. She also rushed pitchers of water to the soldiers, getting her the nickname Molly Pitcher.

The final battle

General Washington's plan was to keep his army moving, hopefully tiring out the British forces. Still, he lost several battles in New York and New Jersey. In October 1777, the Americans won a major battle at Saratoga, New York. Their luck was changing.

The end of the war came with the Battle of Yorktown, Virginia, in 1781. American soldiers, helped by French soldiers, surrounded the British troops there. Guns fired and cannons roared for days. Finally, they stopped. An English drummer boy climbed on top of a hill. He beat his drum. An officer stood beside him waving a white handkerchief. The British were **surrendering.** America had finally won its independence.

► In the Revolutionary War, more than 12 major battles were fought in the colonies. Over 25,000 American and 10,000 British soldiers were either killed or died of wounds, disease, or exposure.

Saratoga Bennington
Bunker Hill
White Plains
Trenton
Brandywine Monmouth
Germantown
Yorktown
Guilford
Court House
Kings Mountain
Cowpens
Eutaw Springs
Atlantic Ocean

N
W E
S

0   125 miles
0   200 kilometers

27

CREATING A NEW GOVERNMENT

When the war ended, George Washington decided to return to his home at Mount Vernon, Virginia. He was 51 years old and ready to spend time improving his plantation and searching for new land to buy. He continued to keep up with the news of the country. Before long, he was quite worried about its future.

The 13 colonies had become 13 **states**. The first **constitution,** the Articles of **Confederation**, loosely joined the states together, but each state really acted like a separate country. Each had its own laws, **taxes**, and money. It was difficult for someone in one state to purchase something in another. It was difficult to resolve problems between states.

George Washington, like many other Americans, feared that the United States might fall apart without a stronger national government. Finally, 12 states sent **delegates** to a **convention** in Philadelphia in May 1781. Rhode Island did not attend.

Washington leads the Convention

At first, George Washington did not even want to attend the Constitutional Convention. He had not been feeling well and his **plantation** needed his attention. His friends persuaded him to be one of Virginia's delegates. At the meeting, the delegates knew they needed a president of the convention to guide them through many difficult decisions. All votes went to George Washington.

▲ The sign of an inn. Inns were set up along major routes as stopping off points for travelers. Here they could get food, drink, and a bed for the night.

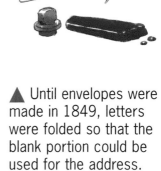

▲ Mail was carried from town to town by post riders. There were no postage stamps. The receiver of the letter paid the rider for it in cash.

▲ Until envelopes were made in 1849, letters were folded so that the blank portion could be used for the address. Edges were sealed with sealing wax.

◀ George Washington—seen here on the right, raising his hat—enters the Constitutional Convention alongside Benjamin Franklin and John Paul Jones. This painting is by J.G. Ferris. Meetings inside the hall were kept secret.

The Constitutional Convention
At the convention, the delegates expected to revise the Articles of Confederation. Instead they decided to write a new constitution for the United States. This divided the national government into three branches. The executive branch was the president and vice-president, who were elected. The judicial branch was the courts and judges. The legislative branch was called **Congress**. It made laws.

◀ On May 25, 1787, 55 delegates arrived at Independence Hall in Philadelphia for the Constitutional Convention. Many people were unsure about the Constitution. Did the president have too much power? Did the states have enough power?

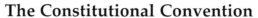

There were two parts to Congress: the Senate and the House of Representatives. Citizens elected **representatives** to Congress. No one branch had all the power. The states still controlled their local governments. This system of national government is still used today.

THE NATION'S FIRST PRESIDENT

In 1789, George Washington went home to Virginia. But he did not get the quiet life he wanted. Instead he was elected President of the United States. He wrote in his diary, "I bade farewell to Mount Vernon, to private life and with a mind oppressed with more anxious and painful sensations set out for New York."

People connected George Washington's name to the new **Constitution**. They knew him as a strong leader and loyal American.

In the **nation's** first **election**, George Washington received the most votes, making him the nation's first president. John Adams received the next highest vote, so he became the vice-president. In April, 1789, both men headed for New York City, the nation's first **capital**.

As Washington's coach traveled from Virginia to New York, crowds waved and cheered in every town along the way. He, his wife, and his grandchildren, moved into the Presidential Mansion. New York did not remain the nation's capital for long. In 1790, the capital was moved to Philadelphia.

▼ A portrait of George Washington by Gilbert Stuart in about 1795. George and Martha Washington had many fancy parties in their presidential mansions in New York and Philadelphia. Every Tuesday afternoon all properly dressed visitors were welcome into their home.

People's rights
In 1791, Congress passed the Bill of Rights. They were **amendments** to the Constitution that protected the rights of the people. Some of these rights included:
• freedom of speech
• freedom of religion
• freedom of the press
• the right to jury trial
• the right to bear arms to protect the government
• in peacetime, the government cannot make people house and feed soldiers
• people or their homes cannot be searched without good reason.

Washington and government

1783 Treaty of Paris ends the Revolutionary War	**1790** Nation's capital moves from New York to Philadelphia
1787 Constitutional **Convention**	**1791** Bill of Rights is **adopted** by Congress
1788 11 states approve the Constitution	**1793** Washington's second inauguration
1789 Washington's **inauguration**	**1796** Washington's Farewell Address.

► A view of City Hall in Wall Street, New York City in 1790. This area became the center of banking and finance in the United States.

▼ On April 23, 1789, Washington paraded into New York City. On April 30, Washington took the oath of office at his inauguration. He promised to "preserve, protect, and defend the Constitution of the United States."

Four more years in office
Congress's job was to make laws. The president had to approve the laws or stop them with a **veto.** The first important law set **taxes** on goods that came from other countries. The taxes would raise money for the government. Washington approved this law. In 1793, Washington was re-elected as president.

WORKING IN THE NORTH

After the war, Americans once again focused on their homes and their work. Many people in the southern states raised crops on large farms, called plantations. There were farmers in the northern states, too, but many northerners earned their livings working in shipyards, grain and lumber mills, and iron furnaces.

A mill is a building that manufactures things. There were saw mills that sawed logs into boards, and grain mills that ground corn and wheat into flour. Mills were usually located by fast-moving rivers and streams because the water provided power for the waterwheel. As water rushed over the wheel, the wheel turned the saw or grinding stone.

Many people ran iron furnaces. They took iron **ore** from the ground and heated it in big furnaces. Much of the iron was sold to other countries. Some of it was sold to local blacksmiths who made farm tools, nails, and parts for guns.

▶ This town looks much like Brandywine Village, Delaware, in the late 1700s. The Brandywine River provided power for the mills. Boats brought corn and wheat from other **states**. After the grains were ground, the flour was put into barrels. The barrels were loaded onto boats. The boats sailed from the Delaware River into the Atlantic Ocean, from where they went all around the world.

▶ George Washington died on December 14, 1799. His wife and grandchildren were by his bedside at the time.

Capital of the states
In 1791, George Washington picked the site of the **nation's** permanent **capital**. The site was on the Potomac River in Virginia and Maryland. The new city was first called Federal City. Later it was named Washington, D.C. (District of Columbia).

◀ The jobs in or near the mills included:
• unloading corn and wheat off the boats from Maryland, Virginia, and New York
• grinding wheal into flour at the mills
• building ships to transport the flour barrels.

▲ Every village had a blacksmith who made useful things, such as tools and horseshoes.

▼ Shipbuilders in Philadelphia in 1798 build a warship for the **navy**. Congress had set up the U.S. Navy in 1794 to protect American ships from raids by pirates and the French. France wanted to stop American trade with Britain. This was because America had not helped France in its battles against Britain in Europe.

Job skills and pay

Busy mills meant more business for the village coopers. A cooper made wooden barrels for storing and shipping flour. Coopering required great skill to shape the barrels and make them watertight. A person learned and practiced that skill by working with an experienced cooper.

In the mid-1790s, a cooper earned about $1 a day. That pay was high compared to a mill worker, who earned about $7 a month. Mill workers, however, usually received free housing and clothing.

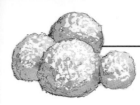

WORKING IN THE SOUTH

"Led by an old driver carrying a whip, forty of the largest and strongest women I ever saw together each having a hoe over the shoulder, and walking with a free, powerful swing." Frederick Law Olmsted traveled through the south in the 1800s. In 1854, he wrote that description of slaves on a plantation.

In the South, there were many **plantations**, or large farms. Many plantation owners grew cotton, which they sold to England to make cloth. A plantation owner could get very rich as long as he had cotton—and **slaves**.

Growing lots of cotton required many workers with strong backs to plow, hoe, and pick the cotton. Plantation owners used African slaves to do this work. Most slaves worked hard all day long. Many were whipped and treated cruelly. Slaves lived in small shacks around the owner's large house. They usually slept on straw or rags on the floor.

Speeding up the work
Many people knew that slavery was wrong. Especially in the North, people spoke out against it. In the South, however, plantation owners thought that slavery was necessary. It would take years before this awful practice ended.

In 1793, a schoolteacher named Eli Whitney invented the cotton gin, a machine that removed cotton seeds from the cotton plant. Now planters could produce cotton even faster and cheaper—all the more reason to own many slaves.

▼ Slaves on a plantation entertain themselves—from a painting by an unknown artist in about 1798.

▲ Plantation owners and their families lived with many comforts, including a large house with many bedrooms.

An end to slavery?
When Americans won their independence from Britain, African Americans hoped that slavery would end, too. In 1799, a group of African Americans sent a **petition** to President John Adams and **Congress**. It asked for an end to the slave trade and for the protection of free African Americans. Congress rejected the petition in a vote of 85 to 1.

▶ A large plantation was like a village. Owners grew enough food for their families. Some slaves became skilled workers for the plantation, such as blacksmiths, cooks, and brickmakers.
1. owner's house
2. owner's yard
3. owner's kitchen
4. ice house
5. kitchen garden
6. slaves' houses
7. barn.

◄ A bell rang a half-hour before sunrise. In a few minutes, slaves were expected to be dressed, grab a quick breakfast, and run to the field. They worked until dark. Then they did their chores, such as tending their gardens.

▲ Eli Whitney's cotton gin removed the seeds from the cotton fibers. The fibers were shipped to England, where they were made into cotton cloth.

PIONEERS MOVING WESTWARD

The new nation was growing. Towns in the East were getting crowded. Americans wanted more land. They left everything familiar and headed west. These people were called pioneers because they were the first settlers in an unfamiliar land.

▼ Daniel Boone led pioneers through the Cumberland Gap, a narrow valley in the Appalachian Mountains. This painting of 1852 is by George Caleb Bingham.

A frontier is the land between a settled area and wilderness. At first America's frontier was the eastern part of Virginia and the other colonies. As these places became settled, it moved west to Kentucky and Indiana. Later, the frontier moved all the way to the Pacific Ocean.

▲ This is a frontier village in Kentucky. Barrels of sugar and flour are unloaded from a wagon outside the general store. Settlers from miles around come to the store to buy, sell, or swap goods.

36

Pushing back the Native Americans

The pioneer spirit was great for the settlers. It was awful for most Native Americans. Many died in battles over land. Others died from disease. Some joined the pioneer communities. The majority were forced to flee farther west.

Tecumseh, a Shawnee leader, tried to encourage Native Americans to fight for their land. He spoke these words in 1810 to the Osage in the Ohio River Valley: "Brothers—the white people came among us feeble; and now we have made them strong, they wish to kill us, or drive us back, as they would wolves and panthers. At first, they asked for land sufficient for a wigwam. Now, nothing will satisfy them but the whole of our hunting grounds, from the rising to the setting sun."

▲ In 1779, an African-American named Jean Baptiste Point du Sable and his Native American wife, Catherine, were pioneers in Illinois region. They built a trading post on the southwestern edge of the Great Lakes, near a river that the local Potawatomi tribe called Checagou. This was the beginning of Chicago.

▲ A frontier family rest beside a stream on the road to Pittsburgh. They are traveling in a Conestoga wagon. In the 1790s, Pittsburgh became the major starting point for pioneers heading west.

THE SPANISH IN AMERICA

When they became states
1787 Delaware, New Jersey, Pennsylvania
1788 Connecticut, Georgia, Maryland, Massachusetts, New Hampshire, New York, South Carolina, Virginia
1789 North Carolina
1790 Rhode Island
1791 Vermont
1792 Kentucky
1796 Tennessee

In 1796, the United States did not fill even half of North America. The nation's western border was the Mississippi River. Most of the land west of the river belonged to Spain. Florida, too, belonged to Spain. Many of these Spanish-speaking people had never heard of the Revolutionary War.

One small piece of the East Coast did not belong to the United States. That was Florida and it was under Spanish rule. Native American groups, such as the Timucua and Seminole, lived in Florida. **Slaves** who escaped slavery in Georgia ran to Florida and hid with the Seminoles. This made Georgia slave-owners very angry. They wanted the United States to take over Florida and permit slaves to be captured there. This did not happen until 1821.

▼ The **mission** of San Carlos de Borromeo was located in present-day California. At this time, California, Texas, New Mexico, and Arizona were all part of Mexico (owned by Spain).

▶ The Spanish often built presidios, or forts, to guard the Spanish missions. These Spanish soldiers are watching over Misión San Francisco de Asis, which later grew into the city of San Francisco, California. The guard on horseback is following Native American workers from the fields back to the mission. The Native Americans could not leave the presidio without permission.

▶ This is Santuario de Chimayo as it is today. In the late 1700s, it was a presidio chapel. Chimayo is near Santa Fe, the capital of present-day New Mexico. This area did not gain independence from Spain until 1821.

▲ In the missions, Native Americans learned to talk and act like Spanish citizens. They were not treated as badly as if they were slaves, but they had to follow many rules and regulations.

Spreading Spanish culture

Spain wanted to hang on to its land in western North America. It built many missions and sent priests and groups of settlers to run them. A mission is a farm or village centered around a Catholic church.

Spaniards brought Native Americans into the missions to live, work, and learn. Many learned skills such as carpentry and metalwork. The Native Americans were expected to join the Catholic religion and become loyal Spanish citizens. This "education" tried to destroy the Native American culture. When Native Americans could not speak their language and tell their stories to their children, their traditions were lost forever.

Many of today's cities began as Spanish settlements. Mision San Antonio de Valero became San Antonio, Texas. The presidio San Diego de Alcalá became San Diego, California.

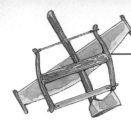

AMERICAN CITIZENS

On March 4, 1801, Thomas Jefferson walked along Washington, D.C.'s muddy streets on his way to his inauguration. There were no fancy parades. Jefferson kept the event simple. He wanted Americans to know that he represented ordinary citizens.

Since the Revolutionary War, Americans behaved differently from Europeans. Visitors from Europe were often surprised by this behavior. In America, equality was fashionable, to a certain extent. People stopped using the word "servants," and instead used "help" or "hired hands." Except in the southern **states**, people stopped using the words "master" and "mistress." Strangers spoke to each other without waiting for an introduction. Strangers even asked each other personal questions. A wealthy man might actually share a meal in an inn with his coach driver.

▲ Thomas Jefferson was the nation's third president and the first one to be **inaugurated** in the new **capital** of Washington, D.C. He was well known for writing the **Declaration** of Independence and the Statute of Religious Freedom, and for his great wisdom.

◀ In the late 1700s, many **elections** were held in open fields. A citizen's vote was not always private the way it is today.

▶ In Philadelphia in 1803, some men hand their voting papers through the windows of Independence Hall (on the right) while others argue in the street.

Who could vote?
1789 white men over age 21 who owned property
1800–1850s all white men over age 21
1870 all men regardless of race or color
1920 all men and women over age 21
1971 all men and women over age 18.

Educated citizens

Thomas Jefferson believed that schools were needed if Americans were to govern themselves. People must know how to read and write. They needed to know how their government worked and what was happening in their world. Whenever the government divided up new land for pioneers, land was set aside for a school.

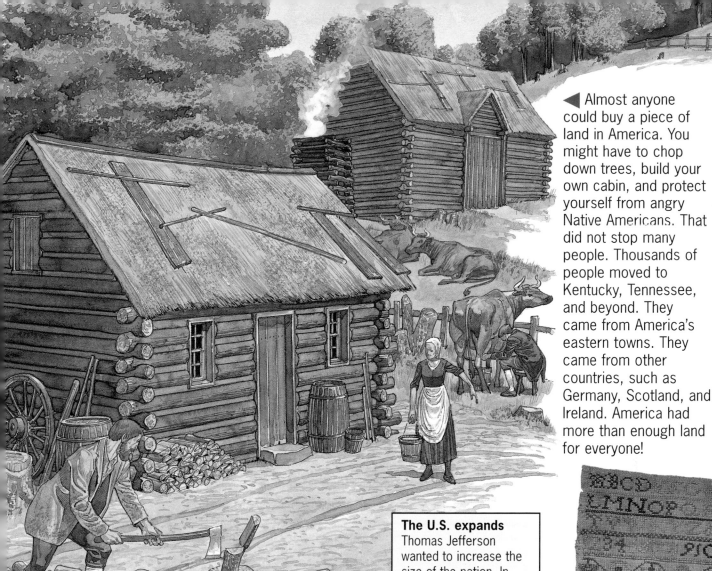

Almost anyone could buy a piece of land in America. You might have to chop down trees, build your own cabin, and protect yourself from angry Native Americans. That did not stop many people. Thousands of people moved to Kentucky, Tennessee, and beyond. They came from America's eastern towns. They came from other countries, such as Germany, Scotland, and Ireland. America had more than enough land for everyone!

The U.S. expands

Thomas Jefferson wanted to increase the size of the nation. In 1803, he purchased Louisiana Territory from France, doubling the size of the United States of America. In 1804, he sent Meriwether Lewis and William Clark to explore the far west.

The end of the Washington era

Martha Washington died at Mount Vernon on May 22, 1802. She had shared the birth of America with her husband. She traveled long distances to join him near the battlefields of the Revolutionary War. She was America's first First Lady.

This needlework panel, showing the alphabet and numbers, was made in about 1800 by a young girl at school.

Counting heads

In 1790, the United States took its first census. That means it counted all its people. There were almost four million people in 1790. Almost 700,000 of those people were slaves. Native Americans were not counted in the census. By 1890, there were 63 million Americans. Today there are about 270 million.

41

Historical Map of America

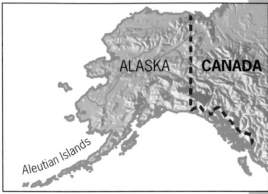

On the map

This map shows North America in 1800. The United States covered less than half of the continent. Spain owned much of the rest. Maine was part of Massachusetts (until 1820). The **nation's capital** had just been moved from Philadelphia to the new city of Washington, D.C. Daniel Boone was exploring the **frontier** along the Cumberland Gap. There were cities on the East Coast and **plantations** in the South. West of the Appalachian Mountains there were pioneer cabins and trading posts. On the West Coast, there were Spanish settlements. Native Americans were being pushed westward.

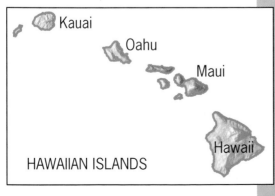

River
English Settlers
French Settlers
Spanish Fort or Mission
Russian Fort

FAMOUS PEOPLE OF THE TIME

Abigail Adams, 1744–1818, was the wife of John Adams, the second president, and mother of John Quincy Adams, the sixth president. She was one of the nation's first supporters of women's rights. She also opposed slavery.

John Adams, 1735–1826, served in the Continental Congress and signed the Declaration of Independence. He negotiated the Treaty of Paris with Britain to end the Revolutionary War. He was the nation's first vice-president and in 1797 he became the nation's second president.

Samuel Adams, 1722–1803, opposed Britain's rule over the colonies. He signed the Declaration of Independence.

Benedict Arnold, 1741–1801, was an American general in the Revolutionary War. Feeling he was not honored for his accomplishments, he later fought on the British side.

Crispus Attucks, 1723?–1770, was an African American leader of the patriot crowd that was fired upon in the Boston Massacre. He was one of the first killed there.

Daniel Boone, 1734–1820, learned from the Native Americans how to survive in the wilderness. In 1769, he led pioneers and settlers beyond the frontier into Kentucky and fought against Native Americans to protect his new settlement of Boonesboro.

Edward Braddock, 1695–1755, was a British general in the French and Indian War. He died in an early battle at Fort Duquesne.

George Rogers Clark, 1752–1818, was an American general in the Revolutionary War and helped win land north of the Ohio River.

Benjamin Franklin, 1706–1790, was sent to London to speak about the colonial resentment of taxation. He received much credit when the Stamp Act was repealed. When the Revolutionary War started, he presented his Plan of Union. He helped draft the Declaration of Independence, the Treaty of Paris which ended the war, and attended the Constitutional Convention. He was also an inventor and publisher.

Thomas Gage, 1721–1787, was a British governor of Massachusetts in 1774–1775. His enforcement of the Intolerable Acts and other harsh treatment of colonists led to the battles of Lexington and Concord and the Revolutionary War, in which he was a general.

IMPORTANT DATES AND EVENTS

GEORGE WASHINGTON
1732 born in Westmoreland County, Virginia
1749 becomes a surveyor
1752 joins the British military in Virginia
1754 begins participation in the French and Indian War
1759 marries the widowed Martha Dandridge Custis
1774 elected delegate to First Continental Congress
1775 elected commander-in-chief of the Continental Army
1781 wins American victory at Yorktown, ending the Revolutionary War
1787 elected president of the Constitutional Convention
1789 elected first president of the United States
1793 reelected to second term as president
1796 refuses third term as president, publishes *Farewell Address*
1799 dies at Mount Vernon at age 67

OTHER EVENTS IN NORTH AMERICA
1754 French and Indian War begins
1759 British capture Quebec in Canada from the French
1760 British capture Montreal in Canada from the French
1762 France gives Louisiana Territory to Spain
1763 Treaty of Paris ends the French and Indian War
1763 Pontiac's War
1765 Stamp Act is passed
1769 Junípero Serra sets up the first Franciscan mission in California, in what is now San Diego
1770 Boston Massacre
1773 Boston Tea Party
1774 Intolerable Acts passed
1774 First Continental Congress meets
1774 The Quebec Act gives French Canadians political and religious rights
1775 fighting at Lexington and Concord; Second Continental Congress meets
1776 Declaration of Independence; Battle of Trenton
1777 Battles of Princeton and Saratoga; France joins American forces against the British
1781 Articles of Confederation are accepted; American victory at Yorktown
1783 Treaty of Paris ends Revolutionary War

King George III, 1738–1820, ruled Great Britain while the colonies in America won their independence.

Patrick Henry, 1736–1799, supported independence for the colonies. He served in the House of Burgesses and Continental Congress, and worked to add the Bill of Rights to the Constitution.

Thomas Jefferson, 1743–1826, drafted the Declaration of Independence. He was Virginia's governor during the end of the Revolutionary War. He became the nation's third president.

James Madison, 1751–1836, made written records of the discussions in the Constitutional Conventional and mostly wrote the Constitution. He became the nation's fourth president.

Thomas Paine, 1737–1809, went to America from England and wrote the pamphlet, *Common Sense*, which encouraged colonists to seek independence.

Molly Pitcher, 1754?–1832, was a nickname for Mary Hays. In the Revolutionary War she helped by carrying water pitchers for the soldiers onto the battle grounds.

Pontiac, 1720?–1769, was a chief of the Ottawa tribe. He tried to unite Native Americans from the Great Lakes area to defend their land against colonists and pioneers.

Paul Revere, 1735–1818, was a silversmith and a messenger for the Sons of Liberty. He warned Massachusetts citizens that "the British are coming" before the battles of Lexington and Concord. He engraved an exaggerated, but famous, picture of the Boston Massacre. His silver tea pots and bronze bells are valuable items today. His house in Boston is now a historic museum.

George Washington, 1732–1799, led the Continental Army, presided over the Constitutional Convention, and became the first president of the United States.

Phillis Wheatley, 1753?–1784, was a slave for a Boston merchant who taught her to read and write. She became the first published African American writer in the United States.

Eli Whitney, 1765–1825, invented the cotton gin, which separated cotton seeds from the plants.

? means that historians are not sure of the exact date.

1784 the colony of New Brunswick is established in Canada
1787 Constitutional Convention meets; Northwest Ordinance sets up government for territories that become Ohio, Indiana, Illinois, Michigan, and Wisconsin
1787 Constitution is accepted
1789 George Washington becomes first president of the United States
1790 nation's capital moves to Philadelphia from New York City
1791 Bill of Rights is passed. In Canada, the Constitutional Act splits Quebec into the colonies of Upper Canada and lower Canada.
1793 George Washington begins second term, or period, as president
1797 John Adams becomes second president of the United States
1800 nation's capital moves to Federal City, later called Washington, D.C. Spain returns Louisiana Territory to France.

CENTRAL AND SOUTH AMERICA
1762 Britain captures Grenada and St. Vincent from the French
1763 Brazil makes Rio de Janeiro its capital
1780–1783 Peruvian Native Americans lead an unsuccessful revolt against their Spanish rulers
1791 Toussaint L'Ouverture leads slave revolt in Haiti against the French
1797 Britain takes Trinidad from the Spanish
1803 Britain acquires British Guiana, Tobago, and St. Lucia

THE REST OF THE WORLD
1756 Start of the Seven Years War in Europe; Britain and France at war in India; China starts to restrict European influence and trade in the Far East
1762 Catherine the Great becomes ruler in Russia
1768–1779 Captain James Cook, a British navigator, discovers Australia and New Zealand and explores Hawaii
1782 James Watt of Scotland invents an improved steam engine that starts the Industrial Revolution; the planet Uranus is discovered
1783 Montgolfier brothers make the first ascent in a hot-air balloon
1784 Britain takes control of eastern India
1789 start of the French Revolution
1796 Napoleon Bonaparte rises to power in France and starts to control much of Europe
1801 Act of Union unites Britain and Ireland

GLOSSARY

adopt accept an idea

amendments changes in a document that become laws

capital city where the government of a state or country is located

claimed announced that something belongs to you or your country

Confederation group of states working together for each other

Congress formal meeting of delegates; the part of the U.S. government that makes laws

constitution set of laws that state the rights of the people and the power of the government

convention meeting

declaration announcement

delegate someone who represents other people

election process of choosing someone by voting

engraving artwork made by cutting into metal, wood, or glass surface

exports goods to be sold to another country

frontier land between a settled area and wilderness

harbor body of water where ships can come for shelter and to load and unload cargo; also called a port

House of Burgesses representative group of law-makers in colonial Virginia

inauguration ceremony to put someone in a position of leadership, such as the president of a country

lithograph print made from a flat stone or metal plate

military having to do with soldiers or war

militia ordinary people who volunteer to be part-time soldiers

minutemen colonial citizens who could be ready to fight "at a minute's notice"

mission settlement of religious teachers, which includes a farm, church, and other buildings

nation the community of people within a country, usually sharing the same territory and government

navy a country's military sea force, including ships and people

ore rock that contains metal, such as iron ore

Parliament law-making body of Great Britain

petition letter signed by many people asking those in power for change

plantation large farm where often cotton or tobacco are grown

protest strongly object to something

redcoats popular name for British soldiers because of their red uniform jackets

repeal officially cancel a law or act

representative someone who acts or speaks for people as laws are made

slave person who is owned by another

person and is usually made to work for that person

smuggle bring goods into a place illegally

state one of the parts of a nation; in the U.S., each state has its own government and laws

surrender give up or admit that you cannot win

tax money that must be paid to a government which is used to run a town, state, or country

treaty written agreement between two countries, usually to prevent or end a war

union joining together, as in states forming a nation

veto power of a president to stop something from becoming a law

HISTORICAL FICTION TO READ

Collier, James. *My Brother Sam is Dead*. New York: Four Winds Press, 1984—Recounts, through the eyes of a young boy, the tragedy that strikes his family during the American Revolution.

Gregory, Kristiana. *Dear America–The Winter of Red Snow: The Revolutionary War Diary of Abigail Jane Stewart*. New York: Scholastic,1996.—Eleven-year-old Abigail details the winter that George Washington and his soldiers brave at Valley Forge.

Hoobler, Dorothy and Thomas. *The Signpointer's Secret: The Story of a Revolutionary Girl*. Morristown, N.J.: Silver Burdett Press,1991—A young girl delivers messages during the Revolutionary War, even to Washington at Valley Forge.

Speare, Elizabeth. *The Witch of Blackbird Pond*. New York: Houghton Mifflin, 1958—While in Connecticut visiting Puritan relatives, Kit Tyler from Barbados befriends a "witch" named Hannah. Kit is later accused of witchcraft and brought to trial.

HISTORIC SITES TO VISIT

George Washington's Estate at Mt. Vernon
P.O. Box 110, Mount Vernon, Virginia 22121
Telephone: (703) 780–2000. This is George Washington's mansion, estate, and burial place.

Independence National Historic Park
3rd and Chestnut Streets, Philadelphia, Pennsylvania 19106. Telephone: (215) 597–8974 Independence Square and other buildings associated with the beginning of the nation.

Boston National Historic Park
15 State Street, Boston, Massachusetts 02109
Telephone: (617) 242–5642.
A 3-mile-long walk connecting 16 historic sites, including Boston Massacre site, Paul Revere's house, and the Old North Church.

Morristown National Historic Park
Washington Place, Morristown, New Jersey 07960
Telephone: (973) 539–2085. Washington's Headquarters and the Historical Museum and Library, Fort Nonsense, and Jockey Hollow encampment.

Hagley Museum and Eleuetherian Mills
P.O. Box 3630, Wilmington, Deleware 19807
Telephone: (302) 658–2400. The site of the original Du Pont cotton mills, estates, and gardens on the Brandywine River.

Mission San Xavier del Bac
1950 W. San Xavier Road, Tucson, Arizona 85746
Telephone: (520) 294–2624. Built between 1783 and 1797 by Franciscan missionaries, the church and school still serve the Tohono O'odham Native Americans.

INDEX

INDEX